Global Cities
BERLIN

Simon Garner
photographs by Miguel Hunt

CHELSEA HOUSE
PUBLISHERS
An imprint of Infobase Publishing

Berlin

Chelsea House
An imprint of Infobase Publishing
132 West 31st Street
New York NY 10001

Library of Congress Cataloging-in-Publication Data

Garner, Simon.
    Berlin / Simon Garner ; photographs by Miguel Hunt.
        p. cm. – (Global cities)
    Includes bibliographical references and index.
    ISBN 0-7910-8846-4 (alk. paper)
    1. Berlin (Germany)–Juvenile literature. I. Title. II. Series.

DD881.G37 2007
943'.155—dc22   2006027346

Chelsea House books are available at special discounts when purchased in bulk quantities for businesses, associations, institutions, or sales promotions. Please call our Special Sales Department in New York at (212) 967-8800 or (800) 322-8755.

You can find Chelsea House on the World Wide Web at http://www.chelseahouse.com.

Printed in China.

10 9 8 7 6 5 4 3 2 1

This book is printed on acid-free paper.

Designer: Simon Walster, Big Blu Design
Maps and graphics: Martin Darlinson

All photographs are by Miguel Hunt (EASI-Images) except 13, 14 left, and 16, by Corbis; and 57 top, courtesy Wilhelm von Boddien.

First published by Evans Brothers Limited
2A Portman Mansions, Chiltern Street, London W1U 6NR, United Kingdom

This edition published under licence from Evans Brothers Limited. All rights reserved.

All links and web addresses were checked and verified to be correct at the time of publication. Because of the dynamic nature of the web, some addresses and links may have changed since publication and may no longer be valid.

Contents

Living in an urban world

Sometime in 2007 the world's population will, for the first time in history, become more urban than rural. An estimated 3.3 billion people will find themselves living in towns and cities, and for many the experience of urban living will be relatively new. For example, in China, the world's most populous country, the number of people living in urban areas increased from 196 million in 1980 to more than 536 million in 2005.

The urban challenge...

This staggering rate of urbanization (the process by which a country's population becomes concentrated in towns and cities) is being repeated around much of the world and presents the world with a complex set of challenges for the 21st century. Many of these challenges are local, such as the provision of clean water for expanding urban populations, but others are global

in scale. In 2003 an outbreak of the highly contagious disease SARS demonstrated this as it spread rapidly among the populations of well-connected cities across the globe. The pollution generated by urban areas is also a global concern, particularly because urban residents tend to generate more than their rural counterparts.

... and opportunity!

Urban centers and particularly major cities also provide great opportunities for improving life at both a local and global scale. Cities concentrate people and allow for efficient forms of mass transportation such as subway or light rail networks. Services too, such as garbage collection, recycling, education, and health care can all function more efficiently in a city.

Cities are also centers of learning and often the birthplace of new ideas, from innovations in science and technology to new ways of day-to-day living. Cities also provide a platform for the celebration of arts and culture, and as their populations become more multicultural such celebrations are increasingly global in both their origins and their reach.

▼ Potsdamer Platz, designed by international architects, is the new heart of Berlin.

A global city

Although all urban centers will share certain things in common, there are a number of cities in which the challenges and opportunities facing an urban world are particularly condensed. These can be thought of as global cities, cities that in themselves provide a window on the wider world and reflect the challenges of urbanization, globalization, citizenship, and sustainable development that face us all.

Berlin is one such city. Situated just 60 miles from the border with Poland, it lies at the heart of the recently expanded European Union. It is the capital of Germany, the world's third-largest economy, and, with a population of nearly 3.3 million people, the largest city in the most populous country in Western Europe. But it is also a city struggling with the challenges posed by its turbulent history.

A youthful city

More than half of the population of Berlin is under 40, giving the city a youthful feel. Politically too, the city is young. It has only been the capital of united Germany since 1990, and its economy, infrastructure, and social makeup are still adapting to the huge changes brought about by German reunification. Nowhere is this more apparent than in the newly fashionable areas of the east, where graffiti-sprayed walls and doorways, poorly lit streets, derelict buildings, and dingy bars rub shoulders with new cafés, restaurants, cocktail lounges, and nightclubs. There are few cities in the world that have changed as fast and as much as Berlin has since 1990.

▲ The Hackesche Höfe, a series of interlinked courtyards just north of Alexanderplatz, are a focus both for shopping and nightlife.

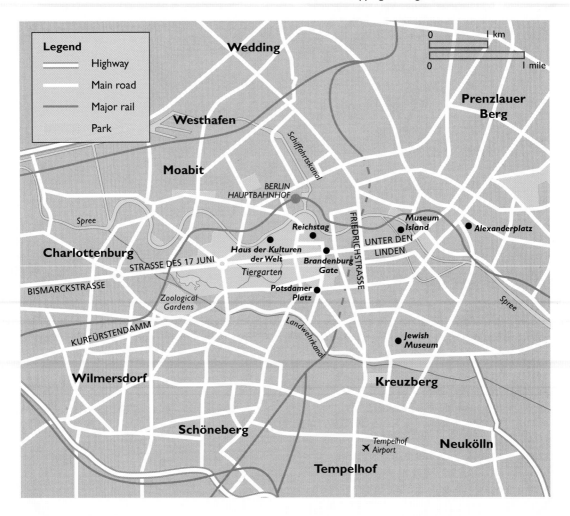

Legend
— Highway
— Main road
— Major rail
  Park

Wedding

Prenzlauer Berg

Westhafen

Moabit

Schiffahrtskanal

BERLIN HAUPTBAHNHOF

Museum Island

Alexanderplatz

Spree

Reichstag

FRIEDRICHSTRASSE

UNTER DEN LINDEN

Charlottenburg

Haus der Kulturen der Welt

STRASSE DES 17 JUNI

Brandenburg Gate

Tiergarten

BISMARCKSTRASSE

Potsdamer Platz

Zoological Gardens

Landwehrkanal

Spree

KURFÜRSTENDAMM

Jewish Museum

Wilmersdorf

Kreuzberg

Schöneberg

Tempelhof Airport

Neukölln

Tempelhof

0   1 km
0   1 mile

A divided city

To understand this transformation you have to look to Berlin's past. Berlin has a history that is unique. For 45 years it was the symbolic focus of the cold war, a metropolis divided through its center by an all but impenetrable 13-foot-high concrete wall (see page 17). On one side of this wall was East Berlin, capital of the communist and totalitarian German Democratic Republic (generally known as East Germany). On the other side was West Berlin, an isolated city of more than 2 million inhabitants, connected to the rest of the Federal Republic of Germany (generally known as West Germany) by restricted road, rail, and air traffic routes.

The challenge of reunification

On November 9, 1989, the Berlin Wall fell. The cold war ended and the two Berlins (and Germany, too) became one again. It was time to look to the future. The city became a huge construction site, with new buildings springing up along the course of the former wall as politicians and developers prepared Berlin for a new role on the global stage as capital of the most powerful country in Europe.

◀ The Urania world clock, in Alexanderplatz, a popular meeting point for East Berliners before reunification. It shows the time in cities all over the world.

The shadow of the past

The people of Berlin, however, do not always share their politicians' optimism. The cost of reunification has driven the city deep into debt, and the city's turbulent history is a warning to residents against expecting too much from the future. For example, Frederick the Great (1712–1786) sought to outdo the French royal palace at Versailles with his castle at Sans Souci, near Berlin; Kaiser Wilhelm II (1859–1941), emperor of Germany, wanted to make Berlin the capital of a colonial power to rival the British Empire; and Adolf Hitler (1889–1945) wanted to turn the city into a monumental metropolis that would dwarf Paris, London, and Rome. Most often it is Berliners themselves who seem to doubt their city leaders' ability to face the challenges of the future.

▲ Large socialist murals such as this can be found in many locations in the former East Berlin.

The history of Berlin

Berlin started life as a small trading post on the marshy banks of the Spree River in the 12th century (the name *Berlin* is thought to come from the Slavic word for "swamp"). In the following centuries it gradually grew to be a small regional capital, but frequent wars, uprisings, and epidemics meant Berlin's development was uncertain and slow.

The Prussians

Modern Germany only came into being in 1871. Before that date the country was split into many small German-speaking states. One of the most powerful was Prussia. It was under the Prussian kings that Berlin first became a significant force on the European stage. Berlin was a religiously tolerant city and the immigration of Jews and Huguenot (French Protestant) refugees was encouraged. These settlers brought valuable new skills and crafts into the city. Under Frederick the Great (1712–1786) Berlin developed into an awesome military power and a cultural and intellectual center with a population of more than 150,000. Prussian military strength, however, could not stop the army of Napoleon I (1769–1821), the militaristic French emperor, from occupying Berlin before he was finally defeated in 1814 and 1815.

▼ The Quadriga (four horses and a chariot) on top of the Brandenburg Gate was taken to Paris after Napoleon occupied Berlin. It was returned in 1814 after he was defeated. Badly damaged in the Second World War, it was replaced in 1958 with the replica seen here.

▲ The statue of Frederick the Great on Berlin's main boulevard, Unter den Linden, commemorates Prussia's most famous king.

Industrialization, urbanization, and revolution

In the early 19th century Berlin led the industrial revolution in Germany. Workers flooded into the city to work in the new factories, often living in appallingly overcrowded conditions. In 1848 the people revolted, demanding political reform and an elected national parliament to unite the separate German states. The revolution failed. The unification of Germany was finally achieved 23 years later, though not as the revolutionaries of 1848 had imagined. The politician Otto von Bismarck (1815–1898) engineered the unification of the numerous states of Germany through the skillful use of diplomacy and military strength. From 1867 he was chancellor (the political leader) of the North German Confederation. This was enlarged in 1871 to become the German Empire, with Wilhelm I, the king of Prussia (1797–1888), declared kaiser (emperor). Berlin was now the capital of an ambitious new political power that sought to rival Russia, Britain, and France.

◀ Bismarck and Prince Heinrich of Prussia reviewing troops outside the imperial castle in Berlin sometime before the First World War.

Imperial capital

Berlin celebrated its newfound status with an explosion of growth and nationalist confidence. In 1871 its population was 826,000. As of 1888, when Kaiser Wilhelm II (1859–1941) came to the throne, it had nearly doubled. By 1910 it was 2 million.

While grand government buildings were erected in the city center, however, the living conditions of the working class worsened. They turned to the new left-wing German Social Democratic Party (SPD) for support. By 1912 the SPD was the largest party in the Reichstag (German parliament). Nevertheless, when the kaiser decided to support Austria and declared war on Russia and France in August 1914, support was virtually unanimous across all political parties.

The First World War

Kaiser Wilhelm II told departing troops they would be home before the leaves had fallen from the trees. They were not. Over the four years of the war huge numbers of casualties mounted at the front. Meanwhile, a continual British naval blockade and a failed harvest left the civilian population starving. By 1918 antiwar feeling had grown rapidly. There were mass strikes, and when the soldiers mutinied, the kaiser was forced to abdicate. On November 11, 1918, an armistice halted hostilities on the western front. In June the following year the warring parties signed the Treaty of Versailles, formally ending the war. It required Germany to give up 13 percent of its European territory, surrender its entire colonial empire, and pay massive war reparations to the allies that had fought against it.

Democracy and decadence

In the aftermath of the First World War, Berlin was politically unstable. The Weimar Republic, Germany's first attempt at democratic government, was established amid violent conflict between radical communists (known as "Spartakists"), the more moderate SPD, and right-wing elements still loyal to the monarchy. Inflation, in part caused by the war reparations, spiraled out of control. By late 1923 one U.S. dollar was worth 4,200,000,000,000 marks. It took a wheelbarrow full of money just to buy a loaf of bread.

Berlin became famous for its outrageous and decadent nightlife even as poverty and social injustice caused rising social tensions. In the global recession that followed the 1929 American stock market crash, nearly a quarter of Berliners found themselves out of work. Street fighting broke out between the communists and the growing National Socialist Workers' Party (the Nazis) led by Adolf Hitler. The people of Germany wanted a change. In July 1932 the National Socialist Party won 230 of the 670 seats in the Reichstag, enough to take power. On January 30, 1933, Hitler was appointed Chancellor of Germany.

▼ A Berlin housewife in 1923 lights the fire for breakfast with several million German marks. It was then cheaper to start fires with the almost worthless money than to buy kindling wood with it.

The rise of the Nazis

Almost immediately the Nazis set about imposing their extreme right-wing ideology on the capital. Berlin epitomized much that they despised, with its decadence, intellectualism, and avant-garde art. Political opponents of the regime were imprisoned. Jewish business were first boycotted, then attacked, and their owners arrested and deported. On November 9, 1938, 24 synagogues across Berlin were set on fire—an event now known as Kristallnacht ("night of broken glass"). In 1939 the Nazis' territorial ambitions led them to invade Poland. In response, Britain and France declared war on Germany. The Second World War had begun.

▼ In the late 1980s the cellars of the Gestapo Headquarters were unearthed on a vacant lot off Wilhelmstrasse. Today the site houses an exhibition about Nazi atrocities called *The Topography of Terror*.

The Second World War

For most people life in Berlin seemed to continue normally, but as the war dragged on there were shortages of food and fuel and sporadic British bombing started to damage the city. Jews and other groups, such as homosexuals, were transported to the extermination camps. In early 1943 the Soviet Union defeated the German army at Stalingrad, with huge loss of life, and the British Royal Air Force and U.S. Air Force began a concerted campaign against the Nazi capital. It was the most intensive bombing campaign of the Second World War: 14,562 sorties were flown and more bombs (36,800 tons of them) were dropped on Berlin than were dropped on the whole of Great Britain during the war.

On the afternoon of April 30, 1945, already surrounded by the forces of the advancing Soviet army, Hitler committed suicide in his underground bunker. On May 2, Berlin surrendered to the Soviets, and five days later the rest of Germany followed suit. The final battle for Berlin caused around 100,000 civilian deaths and killed or wounded more than 304,000 Soviet troops and more than a million German troops. Berlin was devastated, the defeated capital of a defeated nation. More than two thirds of the city lay in ruins.

▲ Affectionately known by Berliners as "the hollow tooth" the Kaiser-Wilhelm-Gedächtniskirche in the heart of West Berlin has been left as a monument to the bombing in the Second World War.

▼ The huge Soviet War Memorial in Treptower Park is the grave of 6,000 Soviet army soldiers who were killed in the battle for Berlin. Stalin wrote the texts on the friezes.

15

Dividing the spoils

In July 1945 the four Allied powers (the United Kingdom, the United States, France, and the Soviet Union) met at Potsdam, 16 miles southwest of Berlin, to put into effect an agreement reached earlier that year at Yalta. Both Germany and Berlin were divided into four zones, but Berlin itself lay deep inside the Soviet-controlled area. West Berlin (controlled by the United States, the United Kingdom, and France) was effectively an island and vulnerable to any restrictions imposed by the Soviets. Tensions were high between the former allies. If a third world war was going to start anywhere, it could well have been in Berlin.

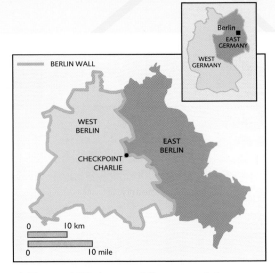

▲ The pre-1989 division of Germany and the route of the wall surrounding West Berlin.

The Berlin airlift

In June 1948 the Soviets cut all road, rail, and canal links in and out of the western sectors of Berlin in an effort to force the western allies to abandon their plans for a democratic state in western Germany. Between June 26, 1948, and May 12, 1949 western Berlin had to be supplied entirely by air. In total 2,236,113 tons of goods were carried by 277,728 flights. At the height of the operation an airplane was landing every minute. Stalin eventually backed down and lifted the blockade, but the lines had been drawn up in what was to become known as the cold war. Vulnerable and isolated, West Berlin was to remain at its heart for the next 40 years. In 1949 Germany was formally divided into two states.

A group of German children stand on rubble in 1948, cheering a U.S. cargo airplane as it flies over Berlin.

The Wall

The most common way for citizens of East Germany (the German Democratic Republic [GDR]) to escape their country's politically repressive communist regime was to cross the border into West Berlin. In July 1961 more than 30,000 East Germans fled to West Berlin, and nearly 22,000 followed in the first week of August. The country was losing its population, particularly young skilled workers and professionals. In the small hours of August 13, 1961, GDR police and troops began unrolling barbed wire along the boundary between East and West Berlin to stop the exodus. West Berlin was encircled in a matter of hours. It was the beginning of the Berlin Wall, a 96-mile-long

▲ This rare remaining watchtower is now a registered historic monument.

construction of fencing and concrete slabs with 302 watchtowers. It remained in place until the revolution that ended communist power in the GDR in 1989.

CASE STUDY

Stefan Leide, Stasi Museum

Stefan Leide is the director of the Stasi Museum. The Stasi was the East German secret police. It is estimated that between 1949 and 1989 the Stasi imprisoned more than 200,000 East German citizens. Of these some 5,000 "disappeared." "In some cases, even today, we still don't know what happened to them," says Stefan. Imprisonment, however, was only one of the techniques used by the Stasi. Both physical and psychological intimidation were common. For example, people who were thought to be a threat to society, perhaps because they knew someone who had tried to leave East Germany, would find their access to higher education restricted, or they might have

trouble at work and be passed over for promotion or lose their job. "The GDR is a recent demonstration of how a government can go bad. We can't change the past but perhaps it is useful to have a bad example. Hopefully, here at the Stasi Museum, we can make people think and be aware of how freedom and human and individual rights can slowly be eroded."

▶ Stefan Leide in the Stasi Museum. The archive contains more than 6 million dossiers—about 112 miles of shelves of documents.

The people of Berlin

The original inhabitants of Berlin were largely Slavic (the name given to some of the Central European peoples), and many settlers came from Germanic tribes expanding eastward. Continual immigration over centuries makes it impossible to define a Berliner in terms of racial origin. But Berliners have developed a distinctive character. They are independent minded and suspicious of authority, and they pride themselves on a robust and irreverent sense of humor known as *Berliner Schnauze* (literally "Berlin gob").

West or East

Despite 15 years of reunification, for many Berliners whether they come from the west or the east is still a defining characteristic. East Berliners, growing up under a communist regime, had very different formative experiences from their counterparts in the west (they will, for example, have learned Russian in school rather than English), and unemployment and poverty is considerably higher in the east. A 2003 survey conducted by the magazine *Stern* revealed the dissatisfaction that continues to be felt by many former East Germans: While 75 percent of Germans in the west were happy with where they lived, in the east only 40 percent were satisfied. A 2006 survey revealed that only a small minority of Berliners had moved from one side of the formerly divided city to the other.

▼ East Germans had to wait years to be able to buy a *Schwalbe* (literally "swallow"), an East German moped. Reunification means that East Berliners can now buy any form of transportation—if they can afford it.

Labor shortage

The construction of the Berlin Wall in 1961 not only physically divided Berliners but also led to a change in the ethnic composition of the city. Prior to its construction, West Berlin had relied on around 50,000 daily commuters from the east who would cross the border each day to work. With this labor supply cut overnight, the West German government looked abroad to fill West Berlin's vacant jobs. Foreign workers flooded in from Italy, Spain, Greece, Portugal, Yugoslavia, and Turkey to take up unskilled jobs. At first they were known as *Gastarbeiter* ("guest workers") and were regarded as a temporary solution, but a vast number of them did not want to return home. Today 13.5 percent of the population of Berlin are of foreign origin.

Becoming German

The long-term integration of immigrant workers and their families into mainstream Berlin society depends on their gaining German citizenship. Up until January 1, 2000, German law stated that automatic citizenship could be given only to individuals whose parents were both German, even if the applicant was born in Germany. Since January 1, 2000, children born in Germany are entitled to citizenship as long as one of their parents has lived legally in Germany for at least eight years. Adults who move to Germany are entitled to citizenship after living in Germany for eight years, provided that they learn German and profess loyalty to the German constitution. These important reforms bring Germany into line with the majority of other European countries.

▼ A kebab shop run by immigrants at Schlesisches Tor, Kreuzberg.

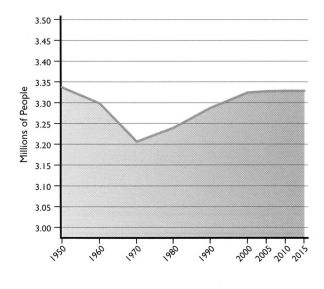

▲ Berlin population changes 1950–2015.

The new Berliners

In West Berlin the largest group of immigrants were from Turkey. They settled in the poorer areas of town, such as Wedding and especially Kreuzberg (see map on page 10), which soon became dubbed "Little Istanbul." More than 119,000 Turkish citizens live in Berlin, and the Turkish community is the largest in Europe outside Turkey.

In communist East Berlin, immigration was far more restricted. East Germany's links were with other communist countries and the largest ethnic minority came from Vietnam to work in the state-owned factories as contract workers. No attempt was made to integrate them into society; they were kept socially isolated and were not permitted citizenship.

When the wall fell, East Germany's Vietnamese found themselves without any legal status in the new Germany, and many were driven into selling cigarettes on the black market. At the end of 2002 there were some 10,000 Vietnamese nationals living in Berlin. They have established a small but thriving community. Vietnamese restaurants are hugely popular among fashionable young Berliners, and a new Vietnamese cultural center has recently opened in the eastern district of Lichtenburg.

Racism

Helmut Kohl, the German chancellor from 1982 to 1998, once famously declared that Germany was not an immigration country. This attitude is still held by some Germans. A recent survey by the University of Leipzig found that a quarter of Germans subscribe to negative views about foreigners and

◀ Every Thursday and Friday on Maybachufer in Kreuzberg, a bustling street market draws Berliners from all over town with its extraordinary prices—the more you buy, the better the bargains get.

immigrants. Such attitudes present some barriers to the integration of ethnic minorities and reflect the fact that these ethnic communities, particularly in the former east, are a relatively new feature of Berlin life. Unlike the United Kingdom or France, Germany had few overseas colonies, so post–World War II immigration to Berlin started considerably later than in London or Paris. More physically threatening is the increase in far-right-wing beliefs among unemployed youths, particularly in the east. Between 1993 and 2003 some 78 refugees died in Germany as a result of racist attacks.

"Multikulti" future

There have been considerable advances in multiculturalism since the mid-1990s, particularly in culture, where a younger generation of Berliners is drawn to the notion of a multicultural society. Books by Turkish-German authors are now frequently found in bookshops, and Turkish-German artists are being welcomed at Berlin's many galleries. Turkish rap and street culture are fueling the Berlin club and music scene, and in 2004, Fatih Akin, a German-Turkish filmmaker, was the first German winner of the Berlin Film Festival since 1986.

CASE STUDY

Asri Sayrac, artist

Asri Sayrac was born and grew up in Istanbul and has lived for 27 years in Germany. A successful artist, he lives and works in a studio in Kreuzberg. "I don't know why racism exists, but I still feel it. And in my first years in Germany I really took racist remarks to heart. But now I have German citizenship and I've found a solution for myself. When you talk to a German you shouldn't speak as an outsider. You should say 'we' and include yourself. Then you are accepted much faster, because in the end it is the Germans themselves who have problems being German. They live with a really terrible past— after all they're just people too— and they miss the freedom other nations have."

▶ Asri Sayrac in his studio. "All my art has to do with the sun. I brought it with me from Turkey. The light here takes the joy away," he says.

The Jewish community

A Jewish presence in the city was first recorded in the official city documents in 1295. In the 18th century under Frederick the Great, Berlin was one of the most open-minded cities in Europe, though this was not what we would call equality today. Jews were still subject to a vast number of humiliating petty restrictions. For example, they were not allowed to enter the city as men and women but had to come in through the gate reserved for livestock and pay a transfer tax like that applied to cattle. By 1910 there were 170,000 Jews living in Berlin, and the Jewish community's contribution to the city both in terms of business and culture was massive. The majority of Jews living in Berlin regarded themselves as assimilated, and many fought for Germany in the First World War.

Persecution

Europe has a long history of periodic discrimination and violence against Jewish communities. The Nazis, however, took anti-Semitism to a new level of horror. On April 7, 1933, soon after taking power, they introduced the "Aryan Clause," a law that prevented Jews from working in the civil service. Further discriminatory laws followed, some petty (Jews were not allowed cameras or pets), and some devastating (Jews were forced to sell their businesses at drastically reduced prices, a process known as "Aryanization"). They culminated with the Reich Citizenship Law in September 1935. This defined citizenship in terms of race, and for Jews, race was defined (illogically, but that didn't bother the Nazis) by the religion of an individual's grandparents. Jews were thus deprived of their citizenship. They had no rights and no recourse to the law. Over the next eight years virtually the entire Jewish population of Berlin was deported to concentration camps, where they were held prisoner and millions were killed. On May 19, 1943, the Nazi propaganda minister Josef Goebbels (1897–1945) declared Berlin *Judenfrei*—free of Jews.

Die Versorgung von Juden mit Fleisch und Fleisch-produkten und anderen zugeteilten Lebensmitteln wird eingestellt.

18.9.1942

▲ Signs on the lampposts in Schöneberg bear witness to restrictive laws against the Jews. This reads: "The supply of Jews with meat, meat products, and other allocated rations is stopped, September 18, 1942."

▶ The graveyard on Schönhauser Allee. Opened in 1827, it is Berlin's oldest surviving Jewish cemetery. In 1943 the Nazis destroyed the nearby cemetery in Grosse Hamburger Strasse, which dated back to 1672.

Jewish Berlin today

Today, Goebbels's terrible boast is no longer true. After reunification the New Synagogue on Oranienburger Strasse was restored, and Berlin has one of the fastest-growing Jewish communities in the world. More than 170,000 Russian Jews have migrated to Germany since 1990 and the majority have settled in Berlin. The new Jewish Museum in northern Kreuzberg attracts nearly 700,000 people a year, among them many young people who want to understand the horrors of Berlin's past. In January 2006 it celebrated its 3 millionth visitor. Its extraordinary building, designed by the U.S. architect Daniel Liebeskind, the son of Polish Holocaust survivors, is world famous.

▶ The Neue Synagogue (New Synagogue) on Oranienburger Strasse was originally built in 1857 in the heart of the old Jewish quarter. Attacked during Kristallnacht and badly damaged by Allied bombing during the Second World War, it is now the center of Berlin's growing Jewish community.

▼ The Jewish Museum in northern Kreuzberg is probably the only museum in the world that was opened by popular demand before it had a single thing in it.

Culture

Berlin has been home to a thriving art and music scene since the 1960s. Because West Berlin was an Allied protectorate, its residents did not have to serve in the national military, as they did in the rest of West Germany. People from all over the Federal Republic came to Berlin to avoid national service. The center of the art and music scene was Kreuzberg. Here squatters took over derelict buildings.

Some extreme elements of this scene turned to terrorism to express their dissatisfaction with the existing political system. Ulrike Meinhof and Andreas Baader's RAF (Red Army Faction) murdered 29 people between 1970 and 1979. Other groups turned to environmental issues and formed a coalition called the Alternative List. The Alternative List won nine seats in the 1981 West Berlin election and developed into the Green Party, which now holds 51 seats out of 614 in the German parliament.

Street life

Berlin is a carnival city. In July 2006 the Love Parade returned to Berlin after two years' absence due to lack of funding. Originally a political demonstration for peace and international understanding through music, the parade became a hugely popular street party attended annually by more than a million people between 1997 and 2000. In May the Carnival of Cultures weekend showcases Berlin's ethnic minorities with a parade and festival. At the end of July the Christopher Street Day Parade celebrates Berlin's gay community; in 2005 it was attended by 400,000 people.

▼ Every May Kreuzberg is host to Berlin's biggest street parade and celebration of multiculturalism: the Carnival of Cultures.

Gay Berlin

Berlin was one of the first cities to address sexual inequality. In the early 20th century Magnus Hirschfeld, an early pioneer of gay rights, founded the Institute of Sexual Research in Berlin and fought against the notorious paragraph 175 of the German Penal Code, which outlawed male homosexuality. In the late 1920s and early 1930s the city's relatively open acceptance of sexual freedom attracted a large number of gay artists and writers from abroad, most notably the English writer Christopher Isherwood. The 1972 film *Cabaret* was based on his Berlin stories.

At around 300,000 people, Berlin has the third-largest gay community in Europe after London and Amsterdam. It is a popular vacation destination for gay people from all over the world, and Berlin (like Paris) is one of the few cities that has an openly gay mayor, Klaus Wowereit.

▲ A juggler practices her skills in Treptower Park by the Spree River. Street performers are a common sight in the city.

CASE STUDY

Josch Luxa and Antje Harms, gay couple

Josch Luxa and Antje Harms are a lesbian couple living in Treptow, in southeast Berlin. Antje is originally from the east and is currently writing her Ph.D. dissertation in computer science; Josch is from West Germany and works in television. Neither of them would consider living anywhere else in Germany. "The best thing about Berliners is that they let you be what you are. They might not always be exactly friendly—and they're certainly not always polite—but they don't disapprove of you. It's a very tolerant city.

▲ Josch Luxa and Antje Harms at home in Treptow.

And though the economic situation can make it hard to get a job you can live well with relatively little money."

Living in the city

Berlin is a city of neighborhoods, each of which has its own particular identity. These range from leafy, sedate avenues to grim former communist housing developments. It is also a city of rapid change. When the wall came down, large areas of cheap housing in East Berlin became available. Berliners quickly took advantage of their sudden freedom to move into, and within, the newly opened east of the city. Shortly after reunification artists, students, and political activists from Kreuzberg moved north and colonized the former workers' quarter of Prenzlauer Berg. There they established trendy bars, restaurants, and clubs.

The broad streets of Prenzlauer Berg are now one of the most fashionable places to live in Berlin.

A city of singles

Only 36.5 percent of the population of Berlin are married, and 50 percent of Berliners count themselves as a single-person household. A high standard of education, relative sexual equality in the job market, and the tendency of many people to put their career first has led to a decline in the traditional family and a willingness to experiment with other forms of living. Many younger Berliners choose not to live alone but in a *Wohngemeinschaft* or WG (literally a "living community"). A WG is basically a shared house or apartment where residents place particular stress upon communal living. Many WGs have a social or political slant—they are often left wing and environmentally aware—and serve not only as a cheap form of housing but also as a way of bringing like-minded people together.

Falling birth rate

The German birth rate has been falling since the 1970s. On average women in Berlin have 1.1 children. This is less than the national figure 1.4 and well below the 2.1 average that is needed to keep the population stable. Some estimates predict that by 2050 more than half the people living in Germany will be over 60. In the long term this will mean that an increase in immigration will be required to fill the job vacancies left by an aging population. In certain districts, Berlin is bucking this trend. In Prenzlauer Berg the number of babies has risen by 24 percent in four years as a consequence of a wealthy, youthful, middle-class population and excellent child care facilities. Many parents make use of state-sponsored day care, but space is limited and waiting lists common.

▶ Only children are common in Berlin, and people tend to have their children later in life. These trends contribute to a declining birth rate and aging population.

CASE STUDY

Giovanni Amandini, fashion designer

Giovanni Amandini is a 36-year-old fashion designer originally from Italy. He lives in Prenzlauer Berg with his German girlfriend and their nine-month-old baby. "We moved here because it was a cheap area to live, but now everything is being renovated and prices are going up." He and his young family are typical of the new creative and cosmopolitan population that have reinvigorated Prenzlauer Berg in the last 10 years. Like many people in the area he is concerned with issues of environmental sustainability. He particularly likes the area because of the ready availability of locally grown food from the many organic shops and markets. "Young people here are looking at things differently. They don't simply want cheap food and are happy to spend a little more for organic produce."

◀ Giovanni does 80 percent of his weekly food shopping at organic shops and markets.

Cost and standard of living

In a recent survey of quality of life in world cities Berlin was ranked 14th, tying with Melbourne; it was 15 places above Paris and 55 above London. In global terms, Berlin is also a relatively cheap city in which to live: In cost of living it ranked 28th in the world while London was second and Paris 17th. Such statistics, however, do not tell the whole story. Though housing is cheap and relatively plentiful, wages are correspondingly low. Monthly earnings per private household are U.S. $1,800 in Berlin, which is considerably less than the German average of U.S. $2,680. And jobs are not easy to find. Unemployment in Berlin is currently running at 20 percent.

▲ The leafy streets and villas of Dahlem are home to Berlin's wealthy elite.

Housing

Berlin was a pioneer in the field of urban housing. In the early 20th century local architects built a number of model housing developments. One example is the Horseshoe development in Britz by Bruno Taut and Martin Wagner. This was functional housing built for ordinary people on modern design principles, and compared with the developments of the 1960s and 1970s it has remained popular. It was a huge improvement over the so-called

Mietskasernen (literally "rental barracks") with their dingy internal courtyards. These tenements were hastily erected in the 19th century to house the huge number of workers that came to the city.

The tradition of innovative housing continues in Berlin. Since reunification some 165,000 residential units have been built or renovated. Many of these have incorporated environmentally friendly features such as insulation, solar power, and combined heat and power (CHP) modules.

The great majority of Berliners rent their apartments and tenants are well protected by the law. Once renters sign a contract on an apartment in Berlin they can stay there as long as they like, provided they pay the rent. A slowly increasing number of people are buying their own apartments, but compared with other cities the numbers are very low. Only 12 percent of Berliners own their own homes.

◄ An unrenovated block in the northern borough of Prenzlauer Berg.

Poverty

High unemployment in Berlin means poverty levels are on the rise. In Germany poverty among children under 15 has risen by 14.2 percent since 2004, and in parts of Berlin it is thought that every third child can be classified as poor. This is, of course, poverty defined in the European way, as people living on less than half the average national income. At the same time the gap between rich and poor is growing: In Germany as a whole 10 percent of the people account for almost half of all net income in the country. At the beginning of 2005 the federal government introduced a controversial and radical reform of social and unemployment benefits (Hartz IV), which effectively reduced the benefit paid to a long-term unemployed person by about a third. The federal employment agency also started to offer so-called one euro jobs. These low paid jobs (between U.S. $1.33 and U.S. $3.70 and hour) allow long-term unemployed people to supplement their benefits and are intended to provide valuable work experience and a route back into the labor market.

▼ The East German housing developments of Marzahn have some of the highest rates of unemployment and poverty in Berlin.

Schools

School attendance starts at the age of six in Berlin and is compulsory for 10 school years. After children attend a common primary schooling, parents have a choice of secondary education. They can send their children to a *Hauptschule* (basic secondary school), a *Realschule* (secondary school with a technical emphasis), a *Gymnasium* (which emphasizes academic subjects), or a *Gesamtschule* (comprehensive school that combines the three other types). Students who successfully complete the *Hauptschule* or *Realschule* may go on to an apprenticeship or a vocational college. Only those attending a *Gymnasium* will take the *Abitur*, the exam that entitles university entrance, though students who perform well at a *Realschule* may switch to a *Gymnasium* at 16.

▲ A classroom at the Eckener-Oberschule in Tempelhof.

CASE STUDY

Jessyca Flemming, school student

▲ Jessyca in her school playground. Her pet rat is named Yo-Yo but she usually just calls him "Rat."

Jessyca Flemming is a student in her fifth year at the Eckener-Oberschule in Tempelhof. She is 16 and currently studying for her intermediate exams in math, German, and English. The Eckener-Oberschule is a *Gymnasium* (grammar school), and Jessyca chose to come here because it is one of the few schools in the area where she is able to study Latin. She doesn't like sport, and her favorite subject is German. Overall she thinks her school is not too bad, though she does notice the effect of the cuts in the education budget. "There are a lot of canceled lessons and sometimes some really bad teachers." The school's student population reflects the makeup of the local area. "This is a racially mixed area," says Jessyca. "In my class there's a Russian, a Pole, an Arab, and eight Turkish students." When she graduates, Jessyca would like to work with animals or be a musician. But she is not optimistic about the future. "There are jobs in Berlin, but unemployment is high and I think it will be difficult to find a career that is reasonably paid." Nevertheless, she loves Berlin and could not imagine living anywhere else. "I've visited a lot of other cities with my mother, and they were nice, but I like Berlin best of all."

▲ Students eat a cheap lunch in the student *Mensa* (the cafeteria) at the Humboldt University.

University

With three large universities and more than a dozen colleges, Berlin is an important center of higher education. There are more than 140,000 students in higher education, and about 14 percent of them are from abroad. The oldest university in Berlin is the Humboldt University, founded in 1810, on Unter den Linden, Berlin's main boulevard. The Technical University in Charlottenburg is Germany's largest technical university. It has nearly 30,000 students, 20 percent of whom are from abroad. Berlin's newest university is the Free University in the western suburb of Dahlem. It was founded in 1948 to serve West Berlin (the Humboldt University was in the Soviet sector). The Free University specializes in the humanities and social science.

Higher education, particularly in science, is vital to Berlin's ability to compete in the global market. Berlin's greatest asset is its young and highly qualified workforce (more than 350,000 people in the city have an academic or technical diploma),

and its future will depend upon utilizing these skills in new science and technology parks at Adlershof and Buch (see page 33).

Health care

Berlin's main hospital, the Charité, is the largest university hospital in Europe. It has more than 3,500 beds and treats more than a million people a year. Health care in Germany is funded by a statutory insurance program to which employees, employers, and national government subsidies contribute. Employees generally pay 6 to 7 percent of their wages in health insurance. But inefficiency and the failure of past governments to restructure the system (one of the most expensive in the world) have meant that for many years the premiums have fallen far short of covering the costs. The system is in debt and a radical reform of health care is one of the government's priorities. But measures to reduce health spending (for example, by introducing prescription charges and ending many previously free treatments) are very unpopular.

▼ Part of the huge Charité hospital complex just north of the Reichstag.

The Berlin economy

From the end of the Second World War to the fall of the Berlin Wall in 1989, Berlin's economy was dominated by the politics of the cold war. Neither the communists in the East nor the capitalists in the West wanted to lose face. National government on both sides of the wall made huge contributions to the city's economy. In West Berlin close to half of the city's budget was made up of subsidies received from West Germany. Not to be outdone, the German Democratic Republic central government concentrated on making East Berlin a socialist showcase.

Bankrupt

Since reunification Berlin has found itself facing some hard economic realities. The cost of reunification, combined with corruption and unrealistic estimates as to how much business the new capital was going to attract, have left the city more than U.S. $61 billion in debt. This is the sort of borrowing more usually associated with a small country than a city. Just paying the interest on this debt requires about a tenth of the city's budget. Since 1995 the city's economy has shrunk by a tenth, largely as a result of the collapse of old and inefficient manufacturing industry in East Berlin.

The effects of this debt are becoming clear to the people of Berlin. Budget cuts mean that retiring schoolteachers are not being replaced, orchestras are being disbanded, the police force is being cut back, and major building projects are being delayed. The problem is made worse by the high unemployment rate, which in turn creates more demands on public spending when the state must pay for the social security benefits of the unemployed. In fact, the debts are so large that cuts alone have no realistic chance of remedying them. The hope is that, if Berlin can at least succeed in bringing its public spending under control, funds will be made available from the national government.

▲ Despite Berlin's dire finances, building work continues all over the city and is a constant source of inconvenience for Berliners.

▲ In an extraordinary building by the American architect Frank Gehry, DZ Bank has showcase offices right by the Brandenburg Gate. The building remains largely empty, however, and the majority of the bank's business is conducted in Frankfurt.

The future

Public spending is not the only measure of a city's economy. In certain sectors there is a strong sense of optimism in Berlin. Geographically it is ideally placed to take advantage of the expansion of the European Union that took place in 2004. It has an excellent communications infrastructure completely rebuilt after reunification, and office space is far cheaper here than in the other major European capitals ($25.19 per square foot as opposed to $107.92 per square foot in the City of London). In contrast with much of the rest of Germany it has a young and highly qualified workforce. The service sector has grown by more than 50 percent since 1989, and,

endowed with three universities and more than 80 state-subsidized research establishments, Berlin is tapping into its large educational resources (see page 31). The Adlershof science and business complex in the southeast intends to become the leading technology park in Europe, and the Berlin-Buch campus of the Humboldt University in the north is specializing in biotechnology and medical science. Since 1998 Berlin's software industry has doubled in size, and the advertising sector has grown 66 percent. In 2004 the city's creative industry as a whole (advertising, media, and design) overtook those of Hamburg and Munich in size.

▲ The construction of Berlin's new main railroad station, Hauptbahnhof, has been up to seven years behind schedule.

◀ Shoppers at the Borsig center. Berlin's expanding retail sector is playing an important role in replacing jobs lost in manufacturing industry.

Manufacturing industry

In the economic changes that followed reunification, Berlin's manufacturing industries were hit hardest of all. Between 1991 and 2003 the city lost more than 400,000 manufacturing jobs, and today only 10 percent of Berlin's workforce are employed in this sector. Siemens is the biggest private employer in the city and the history of the company is part of the history of Berlin—Werner von Siemens founded it in Charlottenburg, one of the outer boroughs of Berlin, in 1847. By specializing in high-quality products and restructuring and expanding its markets abroad (particularly in Asia and the Pacific), Siemens has weathered the post-reunification storm. It is now a global company employing 461,000 people in 190 countries. In 2005 its global sales were worth $90 billion.

CASE STUDY

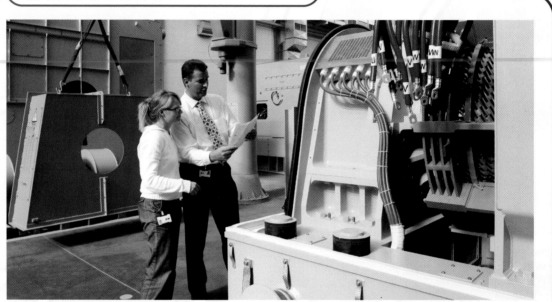

Mathias Mettig, production manager

▲ Mathias Mettig and Sylvia Wittchen check a large electric compressor motor before it is shipped to China.

Siemens's Dynamowerk is situated in Siemensstadt (Siemens City), an entire district of northwest Berlin, including factories and a residential area built especially for the workers. Here huge custom-built electric motors for use in ships, power stations, and steel pressing plants are manufactured. Mathias Mettig is production manager of the Dynamowerk. Sylvia Wittchen is his assistant. "The position of industry in Berlin is certainly difficult," says Herr Mettig. "Berlin is an old city that lived from its industry, and the change to a service economy has seriously affected us." But he is optimistic about the future. "Ten years ago we weren't covering all the world markets, but now we have a good distribution for our businesses worldwide. Today you can do business everywhere in the world. At the moment, 80 percent of our production is for use in China."

Trade

Berlin's future economic success will depend upon trade with the Eastern European markets. Three main rail cargo centers have been built on the outskirts of the city, and it is estimated that by 2010 they will handle 8.8 million tons a year, a large proportion of which will be from Eastern Europe. Shipping is also essential to the Berlin economy. Of the city's 15 public ports, the Westhafen is the largest, linked to the main rivers (the Havel and the Spree) by a 122-mile-long network of canals. In 2004 840,725 tons of cargo passed through these ports.

▼ Barges are loaded at the Osthafen on the Spree River.

Small business

Though Berlin is home to a few large corporations the vast majority of businesses are small to medium-sized concerns. There are only 15 companies in Berlin that employ more than 500 people, and well over 40 percent of the city's gross domestic product is generated by private small businesses employing fewer than 50 people. Low rents, a highly qualified workforce, and support from the Senate department's innovation fund encourage several thousand new companies to start up in Berlin every year. The majority of these are in the service sector, technology, and media.

◄ A worker at the Kryolan theatrical makeup factory in northern Berlin.

Managing Berlin

The city of Berlin is one of the states of Germany, but it is also the capital city of Germany and the seat of national government. Germany is a federal country—it is made up of 16 states (*Bundesländer*), each of which has some freedom to manage its own affairs, such as taxation, education, culture, and policing.

▲ The German constitution, which protects the rights of its citizens, is engraved on a glass wall near the Reichstag.

The structure of local government

The Parliament of Berlin is currently made up of 141 elected representatives. The Parliament chooses the government of Berlin (the Senate), which is made up of the governing mayor and eight senators, all of whom have their own ministerial responsibilities for a policy area. Below the Senate, the city is divided into 12 boroughs. Each borough has its own elected district parliament and district mayor. The powers of the district parliaments are relatively limited and dependent on the Senate, but the district mayors together form the council of mayors whose function is to advise the Senate.

The Berlin Republic

Since 1990 Berlin has been the capital of Germany. The move here from the small, unassuming city of Bonn, a little south of Cologne, was controversial, and the national parliament passed it by only 17 votes. This demonstrates the rather uneasy relationship many former West Germans have with their new capital. Such skepticism is perhaps not surprising given Berlin's history. Berlin is a very different city from small and clean Bonn.

The move is also not complete. A number of major ministries remain in Bonn and the judicial branch of government, the Federal Constitutional Court, remains in Karlsruhe on the Rhine. However, the legislative branch (the Bundestag and

Bundesrat—the lower and upper houses of Parliament) and the executive branch (the Chancellor, Cabinet, and President) have all moved to Berlin. The relocation of hundreds of civil servants to the new capital has provided a major boost to the Berlin economy.

▶ Part of the vast new Spreebogen complex of government offices designed by Axel Schultes and Charlotte Frank on the Spree River next to the Reichstag.

Electoral system

Germany effectively has five major political parties and a personalized proportional representation electoral system. It is rare for any single party to gain an outright majority, so a coalition is usual and smaller parties, such as the Greens, often play a pivotal role in forming the government. The German Green Party's policies are aimed at developing an environmentally sound, sustainable society. Founded in 1980, the German Green Party is the oldest and most politically successful green political party in the world. It holds 14 of the 141 seats in the Berlin Parliament.

CASE STUDY

Claudia Schnatsmeyer, Green Party campaigner

Claudia Schnatsmeyer is a 29-year-old cultural science student in her final year at university. Today is her first day as a Green Party election campaigner but she has been involved in green politics since her childhood. "People in Germany are interested in politics from a very young age. Growing up in the '80s I was very engaged with the ecological movement and experienced how the Greens first made it into parliament." She is campaigning because she wants to make sure the Greens remain in government. "For me they are visionary in many areas of European, environmental, and educational politics."

▲ Claudia Schnatsmeyer campaigning for the Green Party in Pariser Platz.

Policing Berlin

Considering its size, Berlin is a safe place. In Germany, Frankfurt am Main has a higher overall crime rate, and the incidence of street crime and petty theft in Berlin is lower than in several other smaller German cities, such as Hamburg and Cologne. Cuts in public spending have reduced police numbers by more than 3,000 in the last five years, but Berlin still has 17,667 police officers, one for every 186 residents (as compared to one officer for every 220 residents in New York). So far this cut in numbers does not seem to have reduced their effectiveness. Given their numbers, the police generally keep a low profile in Berlin and are only to be seen en masse when one of the frequent political demonstrations goes through the city.

▲ Bundesgrenzschutz officers (paramilitary police who often assist the regular police with public order offenses) caution a cyclist for riding on the sidewalk.

Law and order

In enforcing minor rules—of which Berlin has many—the different branches of the police are assisted by officers from the Ordnungsamt, or Department of Public Order. Ordnungsamt officers wear blue uniforms (the police wear green) and are generally active in enforcing parking restrictions, keeping bicyclists off of sidewalks, preventing jaywalking (it is an offense to cross a street when the crossing light is red), dropping litter or "wild grilling" (barbecuing in a nondesignated area).

The right to protest

Berliners prize the right to protest. Barely a weekend passes without a demonstration of one kind or another. These can take many forms and are often noisy and creative, some focusing on local matters while others take on national or global issues and the international policies of the federal government. New reforms in social and unemployment benefits (see page 29) are a common source of dissatisfaction, particularly among former East Germans. Unemployment in the former east is far higher than in the west, and it is the citizens of the east that will be hardest hit by the cuts.

▲ Turkish women ("Mothers Without Frontiers") protest against the high number of drug dealers at Kottbusser Tor in Kreuzberg.

CASE STUDY

Jens Butner, Berlin policeman

Jens Butner grew up in East Berlin. He originally trained as a mechanic and became a policeman in 1993, a few years after the wall came down. He lives in Prenzlauer Berg and works in the police precinct there. His job usually consists of office work and patrolling in a car, but sometimes he does plainclothes undercover work. "In terms of crime," he says, "Berlin is as safe as any other big city in Germany. The most common crimes in this area are shoplifting, assault, robbery, and theft from motor vehicles." In recent years, though, he has noticed an increase in the use of violence by teenage gangs.

The number of arrests he makes varies. "Sometimes there'll be two on one shift, sometimes only one a week." He considers

police work as a job like any other. "I have to do something for a living—but I also know I'm not able to change the world." He doesn't agree with the cuts to the police budget. "It's a political decision and I don't think it is the right way to handle it. We don't have enough staff or equipment."

▶ Jens Butner on duty in the Prenzlauer Berg precinct police station.

Transportation for Berlin

Years of generous public spending have left Berlin with one of the best city transportation services in the world—it can easily cope with the 2.4 million people it transports everyday. The core of the system is provided by two urban rail systems: the S-Bahn and the U-Bahn. Almost all new expansion projects are suspended, however, due to lack of funds.

Overground/underground

S-Bahn stands for *Stadtschnellbahn* (literally "fast city train"). S-Bahns are larger and faster than U-Bahns and are run by a separate company from the rest of the system. They form the main east-west axis of Berlin's transit system as well as a ring around the center of the city. U-Bahn stands for *Untergrundbahn* ("underground railway") and is equivalent to the London underground or New York City subway. Owing to the difficulties of deep tunneling in Berlin, trains usually run just below street level and often above street level on elevated tracks.

▲ Passengers alight from an S-Bahn at Alexanderplatz station.

Streetcars and buses

In eastern Berlin an extensive streetcar network augments the rail system. Berlin was a pioneer of electric transportation. The first electric streetcar in the world ran here in 1881. Today there are two types: the older Tatra vehicles and newer low-floor models that have easier access for wheelchairs and strollers. In the west, however, the old streetcar routes were dismantled in the 1950s in favor of less environmentally friendly buses. Berlin now has some 161 bus routes.

◀ A Tatra streetcar drops passengers at Alexanderplatz in the center of Berlin.

Traveling outside the city

Berlin is well served by rail, with high-speed trains linking it to most other major German cities. Berlin's new main station, Hauptbahnhof, just across the river from the Reichstag, opened in 2006. This new station allows much easier rail access to the city from both western and eastern Europe. The station building project had been hit by constant delays and cutbacks since it started—the original projected date of completion was 1997. It is now the largest multilevel station in Europe and allows trains to run through Berlin both from north to south and from east to west. It can handle more than 50 million passengers a year, and it generates its own electricity: 780 solar modules are built into the glass roof.

Tegel is Berlin's busiest airport. In 2003 it handled only 11,027,000 passengers and ranked 23rd on the list of Europe's most-used airports. Neither Schönefeld nor Tempelhof, the other two Berlin airports, even made the top 25.

Construction of a new international airport, Berlin Brandenburg International Airport, is now underway on the the site of existing Schönefeld. The new airport should dramatically reduce noise pollution in the center of the city, benefit the economy through increased flights, and provide a new source of employment—the increase in air traffic is expected to create about 40,000 jobs.

▼ Currently Berlin's largest airport, Tegel, is due to close within the next 10 years, when all air traffic will be moved to the Schönefeld site.

Bicycle city

Berlin is a remarkably bicycle-friendly city. It has very few hills, the streets are wide, and it has around 466 miles of dedicated bicycle paths, many of which are separated from the road and have special traffic signals just for cyclists. The city is particularly advanced in integrating bicycling with the public transportation system. Bicycles are welcome at any time of day on the S-Bahn, U-Bahn, regional trains, and streetcars (provided they have a ticket and travel in the designated compartments) and also on night bus services. Cycling in the city is actively promoted by the Senate Department. In 2004 it set up the Bicycle Council (The FahrRat) which has developed the Berlin Bicycle Transportation Strategy. For many Berliners the bicycle is already a real alternative to using a car. Currently 10 percent of all journeys in the city are made by bicycle. The Bicycle Transportation Strategy's goal is to increase this share to 15 percent by 2010. The world's largest bicycle rally (the Sternfahrt) takes place annually in June. In 2005 250,000 cyclists using 17 routes rode into Berlin and gathered at the Brandenburg Gate.

It is not just Berliners who travel by bicycle. There are some 15 or so bicycle rental shops in Berlin, and a number of companies offer organized bicycle tours of the city. For those who don't want to pedal themselves, there are also velotaxis (bicycle rickshaws) available for hire.

◄ Tourists on a bicycle tour visit the surviving section of the Berlin Wall on Niederkirchnerstrasse.

Streetcar 12%
U-Bahn 35%
Bus 30%
S-Bahn 23%

Public transportation 27%
Motor vehicle 41%
Foot or bicycle 32%

▲ Berlin transportation, by percentage.

Road traffic

An efficient road system and relative ease of parking mean that it is hard to persuade Berliners to abandon motor transportation. But only half the households in Berlin own a car. Cleaner and more efficient cars have meant that air pollution from traffic has sunk since 1990, but at the same time traffic's contribution to global warming has risen by 12 percent. For overall levels of pollution to fall, Berlin must reduce the number of cars on its roads.

Car sharing

One way of reducing the number of cars on the roads is car sharing. Greenwheels, Germany's first car-sharing program, was set up in Berlin back in 1988, and the program now has over 100 vehicles that customers can collect from 48 car-sharing stations in the city. Monthly membership in Greenwheels costs $12.25. Customers book on the Internet and pay $3.65 an hour when they use a car (plus 12 cents for every kilometer driven, or about 20 cents a mile). New regulations in two of Berlin's boroughs permitting street stations (like taxi stands) mean the program is rapidly expanding. Greenwheels had 100 new stations by the end of 2006. They estimate that for each car-sharing vehicle, five private cars are taken off the Berlin roads.

CASE STUDY

Katherina Kroll and Wolfgang Wullhorst collect their rental bicycles at Potsdamer Platz station.

DB Bikes

Katherina Kroll and Wolfgang Wullhorst live in Brandenburg, about an hour from the city center. When they come into the city they usually use the bicycle rental system of Deutsche Bahn (DB), the German railroad. These specially designed rental bicycles, complete with lights, lock, and child seat, can be found at most street junctions and stations. If the green light on the lock is flashing, the bicycle is free. Call the number on the bike and you are given a code to unlock it. "Not only is it environmentally friendly, it's fast and practical. It's a good service that is easy to use once you know how," says Katherina.

Wolfgang often uses the bicycles when he is in a hurry to get to a meeting. "I work for DB and get a discount rate. It costs me only four cents a minute. It costs the public seven cents a minute. That's pretty cheap. And if you ride fast, you can save yourself money."

Culture, leisure, and tourism

Berlin has more than 170 museums. These range from the world-class collections of antiquities in the Pergamon and Altes Museum, and of modern art at the Hamburger Bahnhof and the new Berlinische Galerie, to smaller, niche museums often dedicated to a particular artist or subject. The wealth of culture in Berlin is in part a legacy of the cold war. When the city was divided, the original museums were mostly on the eastern side of the Wall, so West Berlin authorities built new museum complexes in the Kulturforum near Potsdamer Platz and in Dahlem. When Berlin was reunified it had two of everything, leading to painful funding decisions about what to keep.

▲ Tourists and Berliners join the long lines for the Goya exhibition at the recently restored Old National Gallery on Museum Island.

Classical music

Berlin is arguably the world's premier city for classical music. It has six orchestras and three opera companies. The Berlin Philharmonic is one of the most prestigious orchestras in the world. Its British director, Simon Rattle, seeks to involve people from all backgrounds in classical music. In 2003 he worked together with a cast of 250 young people from 25 nations drawn from some of Berlin's most disadvantaged suburbs—most of whom had no experience of dance or classical music—to stage a dance performance of Stravinsky's *Rite of Spring*. Berlin is a world center of contemporary dance and it attracts adventurous choreographers from many different countries. The city provides choreographers with some dramatic and unlikely settings for their performances too, such as old factories, World War II bunkers or abandoned subway stations.

◄ In the summer months Berlin offers a broad range of open-air concerts. This one, of Celtic influenced classical music, is on Museum Island.

Memorial city

Besides its museums and culture, the traumatic history of Berlin is also a major factor attracting visitors to the city. It is a sobering place where the scars of the Second World War and a repressive totalitarian regime can still be seen. You cannot go far in Berlin without coming across a reminder of its horrific past or a memorial to those persecuted. The most recent addition is the vast Holocaust Memorial, just south of the Brandenburg Gate,

which was opened to the public in 2005. Underneath the 4.7 acre (204,440 square foot) field of 2,700 stone pillars, an information center invites visitors to inform themselves about the Holocaust and to learn from the mistakes of the past.

► Just south of the Brandenburg Gate, the vast memorial to Jews murdered in the Holocaust opened to the public in 2005.

CASE STUDY

▲ Mr. and Mrs. Hopkins in Breitscheidplatz in western Berlin.

Maureen and Malcolm Hopkins, tourists

Maureen and Malcolm Hopkins are from the United Kingdom but now live in New Zealand. Between 1956 and 1958 Malcolm was stationed in Germany with the British army. "When I was here it was before the wall, and we walked through the Brandenburg Gate—but you had to be in uniform," he says. He has come back to see what Berlin is like today. It is Maureen's first visit, and though she is not really a city person she is impressed by Berlin. "There are so many green spaces around the center," she says. "Most other cities around the world don't have that."

A party capital

Berlin's reputation for nightlife is long standing. All tastes of music are catered to and the ready availability of old industrial buildings in Berlin makes for often quirky and interesting venues.

Berlin is a remarkably outdoor city. At the first hint of summer Berliners take to the streets, swarming outside cafés, enjoying barbecues in city parks, and even stripping off entirely at one of the nudist beaches on the Wannsee or Müggelsee (the large lakes to the east and west of the city).

▲ Berlin has seven beach bars along the banks of the Spree. This one in Monbijou Park is in the heart of the city, opposite Museum Island.

Music and film industries

▲ Film crews are a common sight on the streets of Berlin.

A thriving young music industry has developed out of Berlin's fashionable club scene. Berlin has more than 50 small independent record labels and 80 production companies. In 2002 Universal Music moved its German headquarters here, and it now employs about 500 people in its offices in an old cold storage depot by the Spree River.

Berlin is also a popular location for shooting films, and about 300 are produced in the city each year. Much of this takes place at the old UFA film studios in Babelsberg, where classic early German films such as *Metropolis* were filmed in the 1920s. Berlin's annual international film festival is one of the most prestigious in Europe.

▲ Berlin's basketball team, ALBA, plays at Max-Schmeling Halle.

Sports

Soccer is the most popular spectator sport in Berlin, and most Berliners are supporters of Herta BSC, though some stay loyal to the old East Berlin team FC Union. The World Cup of 2006 was hosted by Germany, with the final in Berlin. The impressive stadium was originally built for the 1936 Olympics and is now home to Herta BSC. It has been completely restored and fitted with a magnificent new glass roof and is ready to face the next 70 years. Basketball is very popular. Berlin's team is called ALBA, named after its sponsor, a waste-disposal and recycling company. Berlin also has a football team, Berlin Thunder, and the Berlin Eisbären (polar bears) are probably the most famous ice hockey team in Germany.

For those who want to participate in sports themselves, Berlin has nearly 2,000 sports clubs, more than 100 public swimming pools, and 16 golf courses. The Berlin marathon takes place every September.

Tourism

Tourism is making an essential contribution to Berlin's economic recovery, and in contrast to tourism in the rest of Germany it is increasing. For Germans Berlin is the number-one tourist destination inside Germany, but still more needs to be done to draw in international tourists. In 2005 the number of people visiting Berlin from abroad increased by 19 percent, but despite this rise the city has too many hotels for the number of visitors it receives. This is good news for tourists—it keeps the prices down—but not so good for hoteliers who are struggling to make ends meet. The 2006 World Cup introduced many new people to the city and is anticipated to provide a long-term boost to tourism in Berlin.

The Berlin environment

Berlin is a wide and open city. In area it covers 344 square miles. The population density is 9,843 people per square mile. Parks and woodland make up 29 percent of Berlin, nearly 7 percent is lakes and waterways, and 5 percent is agricultural land. To the west is the Grunewald, a large forested area containing the Teufelsberg ("Devil's Mountain"), Berlin's highest hill. It is made from the rubble from the houses bombed out in the Second World War. Nearby are the beaches on the Wannsee lakes. To the east the largest lake is the Grosser Müggelsee, and beside the Brandenburg Gate the Tiergarten provides a green space right in the center of the city. Berliners make full use of these outdoor spaces. On weekends they are crowded with walkers, Rollerbladers, joggers, and cyclists.

▶ The lakes in the Grunewald are only a short U-Bahn or S-Bahn ride from the city center.

Berlin soil

Since reunification Berlin has been full of building sites, but building is not easy in Berlin—the city is built on sand and has a high water table. Dig down a few meters and the hole will fill with water. During the construction of Potsdamer Platz some contractors actually used divers to lay the foundations of the new buildings. A further hazard is the remnants of the Second World War. It is estimated that there are about 2,000 unexploded bombs lying in the Berlin soil. A permanent bomb disposal squad is always on call, and they dispose of around 44 tons of munitions every year.

◀ Near any construction site you will find a network of large pink and blue pipes pumping the water back into the nearest river or canal.

Gardens for the gardenless

A peculiar feature of the Berlin environment is the large number of *Schrebergärten* (allotment) colonies. These exist all over Berlin, sometimes quite close to the center but most usually filling vacant patches of land along railroad tracks and major roads. The allotments are large: They usually have a small summerhouse, a vegetable garden, and a lawn. For Berliners, the majority of whom live in apartments, they are an essential part of city life. *Schrebergärten* colonies have also played a significant role in the city's social history. In the recession of the 1920s, when unemployment rendered thousands homeless, these people often moved to the colonies, creating communities and growing their own food to survive.

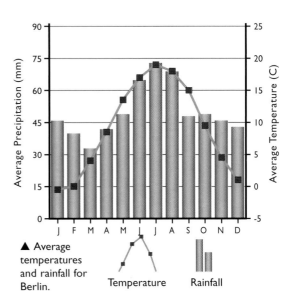

▲ Average temperatures and rainfall for Berlin.

Temperature   Rainfall

CASE STUDY

Wolfgang and Angelika Jahns

Wolfgang and Angelika Jahns live in the western district of Charlottenburg. They have had their *Schrebergarten* for 26 years. "When you have a *Schrebergarten*," says Angelika, "it is like being part of a big family. There are 220 *Schrebergärten* here and we know people from all over the colony." From May to September they live full time in the summerhouse they built themselves with help from friends. "There's always something to do," says Wolfgang. "It's like a hobby. Mainly we grow flowers and vegetables, but if the weather is bad we work on the summerhouse."

▶ Wolfgang and Angelika Jahns in their Charlottenburg *Schrebergarten*.

Protecting the Berlin environment

The German Federal Government is one of the most environmentally conscious in Europe. Two important measures have been ecological tax reform and reducing carbon dioxide emissions. The Ecotax increases tax on fuel and energy while using the money raised to contribute to the public pension program and lower labor costs. Recent studies estimate that since its introduction in 1999 the Ecotax is responsible for a reduction of 2.4 percent (about 22 million tons) of carbon dioxide emissions a year and has created some 250,000 jobs. It has also served to encourage the development of technical innovations in energy conservation, such as energy-efficient housing, low-energy lighting, insulating glass, and natural gas–powered vehicles.

▼ Berlin's lakes are more than a recreational resource. Berlin is the only major city in Germany that can meet its drinking water needs from its own groundwater.

Conserving Berlin's energy

In contrast to the majority of large cities, Berlin has a history of energy conservation. When the city was divided, West Berlin was also separated from the national grid and was forced to become self-sufficient in energy. As a result, West Berlin developed the largest district heating system in Europe: A large central boiler provides economical heat to a whole area of the city.

◄ A modern power station in the northern borough of Wedding.

An environmental success story

After reunification Berlin was confronted with new problems. Much of the energy in East Berlin was provided by inefficient brown coal, or lignite. Brown coal has high ash content, so more must be burned to get the same level of energy as ordinary bituminous coal. This in turn increases the amount of carbon dioxide produced.

In 1994 the Senate for Urban Development set up the Berlin Energy Program with the ambitious goal of reducing the city's carbon dioxide emissions by 25 percent of their 1990 levels by 2010. By 1998 Berlin had successfully reduced carbon dioxide emissions by 18 percent against 1990 levels. This was achieved by a combination of measures: first, a large-scale switch from brown coal to natural gas in both domestic heating and energy production; second, the modernization of old housing, particularly the poorly insulated apartment buildings in East Berlin; and third, the promotion of renewable energy. Good planning does not account for all of the reduction, however. Part is also due to the post-reunification decline of manufacturing industries in Berlin.

▲ At Helene-Weigel-Platz in Marzahn solar panels have been fitted to a newly renovated and insulated East German apartment tower. The solar plates are either side of the central balconies.

Solar energy

Berlin has chosen solar power as its main source of renewable energy. The Solar Initiative of Berlin Business requires solar panels to be used in 75 percent of all new buildings built in Berlin, and the city government subsidizes solar panels for residential housing. Any surplus power can be sold to the national grid at a rate fixed by law. So far 452,000 square feet of solar panels have been installed in the city.

▲ The Ilsenburger recycling center is one of the 15 centers in Berlin that accept environmentally harmful waste.

Recycling

The German record on recycling is remarkably good. Germans generate more waste per capita than any other large European country (1,407 pounds), but in 2003 only 19.9 percent found its way into landfill sites (it was 46 percent in 1995), and 22.9 percent is incinerated. The rest is mostly recycled.

By law, there is a deposit on the majority of both glass and plastic bottles, repayable when the empty bottle is returned to the store. Plastic bags must be paid for, so most people use reusable canvas bags for their shopping. Stores selling large items such as electronic equipment or furniture usually have facilities to recycle the packaging before customers take their purchase home. The trash collection areas of most apartment buildings have separate containers for paper, packaging, glass, and organic waste, so trash is already sorted before it is collected. Berlin has more than 15 recycling centers that will accept more environmentally harmful waste such as batteries, metal, chemicals, old tires, CDs, electronic equipment, and oil.

▶ The mirrored cone in the Reichstag dome, designed by Sir Norman Foster, ventilates the hall below.

Leading by example

Some of the most environmentally friendly buildings in Berlin are government buildings. The newly remodeled Reichstag, for example, has its own CHP (combined heat and power) source fueled by bio-oil. The innovative mirrored cone in the building's dome ventilates the hall below by means of thermal lift as well as providing lighting. The Reichstag is also able to store the heat created when generating electricity and use it later when it is needed. Next door, the brand-new governmental administrative building Paul-Löbe-House has 35,000 square feet of flexible solar panels on its roof that can be angled toward the sun. When they can't generate enough electricity, the Reichstag's CHP source makes up the difference.

A number of projects have been undertaken to illustrate how inefficient East German housing blocks made of prefabricated concrete panels can be refitted and insulated. A particularly good example is at Helene-Weigel-Platz in Marzahn where 480 solar plates have been fitted to the south-facing wall of a renovated East German tower block.

Berlin's ecological footprint

Berlin is a city, and cities eat up a disproportionate amount of natural resources. This consumption can be described as an ecological footprint, measured in global hectares—the area of land required to support one person. (The measure 1 hectare equals 2.47 acres, or 107,593 square feet.) As cities go, Berlin is better than most. Its good recycling record positively influences its footprint, and 90 percent of the food consumed in Berlin comes from Germany. Traffic, on the other hand, was a heavy negative contributor and unnecessary in a city with such a good public transportation system. Berlin's ecological footprint covers an area equivalent to the size of former East Germany.

▲ Locally grown vegetables from Brandenburg on sale at an organic market.

▼ Ecological footprints, in hectares per person, of major cities, Germany, and the world average.

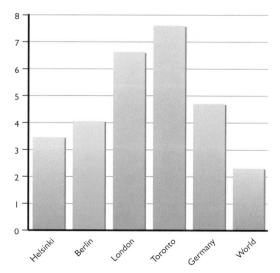

Squatters

Berlin has a wealth of abandoned buildings that squatters have put to alternative purposes. One such example is the Tacheles. Shortly after reunification a collective of political activists and architects squatted the vacant department store on Oranienburgerstrasse. It is now a center for "creative art and living," containing studios, exhibition space, a cinema, a theater, and a café. It is a landmarked building and receives a grant from the Berlin government. However, in a deal with the city, a property developer bought the building in 1997. The artists were allowed to stay, paying a token rent of 60 U.S. cents, until 2008. Farther south in Kreuzberg the Bethanian arts center occupies an impressive 1874 hospital that was saved from demolition by squatters back in 1974. It now offers an extensive residency program for international artists with the emphasis on promoting contacts with Eastern Europe. In the summer its courtyard is home to a large open-air movie theater.

▶ One of the artists in residence at the Tacheles art center.

The UFA Fabrik

In terms of environmental protection, the UFA Fabrik in Tempelhof is the most interesting of these former squats. In 1979 a group of about 100 people took over this abandoned film copy factory (Fabrik means "factory") and embarked on what they termed "an experiment in urban life." The UFA Fabrik boasted the first CHP system in Berlin. It was made out of an old truck engine and named the "Mao-Diesel" after China's communist leader.

◀ Children at the UFA Fabrik's alternative primary school.

Today about 30 people live in the UFA Fabrik. It employs more than 200 more and attracts more than 200,000 visitors a year. Its solar panels supply enough electricity to power the whole community; it has green roofs (covered with soil and planted with grass), a rainwater collecting system, an organic bakery, and a natural food store.

▶ The signs are made by the children at the UFA Fabrik's alternative primary school. They read: freedom, tolerance, friendship.

CASE STUDY

▲ Michael La Fond on the roof of the UFA Fabrik.

Michael La Fond, UFA Fabrik

Michael La Fond is originally from Seattle. He first came to Berlin in the late 1980s and was fascinated by the city. He came back here to study in the 1990s and eventually decided to stay on as the head of the id22, the institute for creative sustainability at the UFA Fabrik. "Our basic philosophy here is that there is more truth in an hour of action than there is in years of talking. For example, we discovered that when you combine solar panels and green roofs, the solar panels work better because the plants reduce the air temperature under the panels. You wouldn't find that out in an academic situation." The UFA Fabrik is also concerned with communication and forging links with the local community. They run a range of initiatives for immigrants, youths, single mothers, and the unemployed. They also are home to a primary school and a children's circus school and hold regular variety and cabaret performances.

The Berlin of tomorrow

Berlin has been through massive changes in the last 16 years. The huge cost of reunification has left the city bankrupt and struggling economically. Berlin's project for the next 15 years is to transform itself into a city able to compete in the world market.

The future heart of Berlin

In 2006 demolition work began on the Palace of the Republic, the old East German parliament building. This building was erected on the site of the original Berliner Stadtschloss (the old city palace) in the city center. The East German authorities had demolished the Schloss, which had partially survived the war, in 1950. Soon after reunification a fierce debate started: What should the site look like in the future? In 1993 the promoters of rebuilding the Schloss showed Berliners one possible future for the center of their city by erecting a huge scaffolding and canvas mockup of the old façade. Many East Berliners objected strongly and regarded the demolition of the Palace of the Republic as just another way in which rich westerners were slowly eradicating all traces of the Democratic Republic.

▼ The Palace of the Republic, a forlorn hulk in the center of Berlin, before demolition work began. The building was closed shortly after reunification to remove dangerous asbestos and was stripped of its original cladding.

Wilhelm von Boddien, Schloss campaigner

Wilhelm von Boddien is the director of the campaign to rebuild the Schloss. "We want to make the heart of Berlin intact again," he says. "If you look at the other historic buildings—the Opera, the Cathedral, the University, the Historical and the Old Museum—you can see they were all built in relation to the Schloss. If we put back the Schloss the relationship between these buildings will be restored and they will

▲ Wilhelm von Boddien, the director of the campaign to rebuild the Stadtschloss, in front of a scale model of Berlin's city center at the end of the 19th century.

recover their dignity." Inside the rebuilt façade the Humboldt Forum is planned, a huge museum of non-European art and culture. If funds can be secured and the project goes ahead, Wilhelm's ambition is to open the rebuilt Stadtschloss on October 3, 2015, on the 25th anniversary of reunification.

◄ The original Stadtschloss in the early 20th century.

Merger of Berlin and Brandenburg

The new airport, Berlin Brandenburg, is to be built on the border between the two states of Berlin and Brandenburg as a joint project (see page 41). In the future there may be more of such projects—a merger between the states has been proposed because currently both states are too poor to function separately. The people must agree to a merger, however. In a 1996 referendum the people of Berlin accepted the idea, but the people of Brandenburg rejected it. If the next referendum is successful the states could merge in 2009.

The future

Berlin is a city of huge potential. It has low property prices, room to expand, and an excellent geographical location. Its greatest asset is its innovative and highly qualified young population. But differences in wealth still divide the city's population, despite the destruction of the wall. The optimism of the planners is not always shared by immigrant communities and the long-term unemployed. Berlin's challenge for the future is to make the most of the city's resources and build a sustainable global city for all its citizens, while controlling and reducing its currently crippling level of debt.

Glossary

anti-Semitism A strongly held prejudice against people of Jewish origin.

biotechnology Technology based on biology and used in medicine, food science, and agriculture.

cold war The tense political situation that existed between the Soviet Union and the United States from the end of the Second World War to 1990.

executive Relating to the part of government concerned with putting laws into effect.

Gastarbeiter The German word used to describe temporary immigrants to Germany who were not granted citizenship; literally "guest worker."

globalization The process of opening up trade and financial markets to allow them to operate internationally.

immigrant A person who lives and works in a country different to that of their birth.

industrialization The process of changing from an agricultural or craft-based economy to one based manufacture of goods in factories.

infrastructure The basic services and physical structures essential to a city, such as water and power supplies, roads and transportation and communication systems.

legislative Relating to the part of government concerned with making laws.

multicultural Involving many racial groups, nationalities, and cultures.

national service A limited term of military service that young adults are required by law to perform for their country; conscription.

proportional representation An electoral system in which each political party receives a number of legislative seats corresponding to the number of votes its candidates receive.

retail industry The service industry involved in the selling of goods to the public.

reunification The joining together again of two things that have been separated. In Germany reunification refers particularly to the reuniting of East and West Germany after the fall of the Berlin Wall in 1989.

Schrebergarten (plural, *Schrebergärten*) The German word for allotment, an area of land in a town or city that a resident can rent to grow vegetables.

service industry The part of an economy that provides services for people and companies such as taxis, banks, and stores, rather than producing physical goods; sometimes called tertiary industry.

Slavic The name used to describe a large group of Eastern and Central European peoples including the Russians, Ukranians, and Poles, who speak any of a set of related languages.

Stasi The East German secret police, formally called the Ministerium für Staatssicherheit (Ministry for State Security).

sustainability The capacity of a lifestyle to preserve the world for future generations.

urbanization The movement of people from rural to urban areas.

Further information

Useful Web sites

Berlin.de
http://www.berlin.de/english/index.html
The official Berlin portal, with information on tourism, government, and business in the city.

Berlin Tourismus Marketing
http://www.berlin-tourist-information.de
The English-language Web site of Berlin's official tourist board. It provides much up-to-date information about what is happening in Berlin and includes a section for young people, "Bock auf Berlin."

Senate Department of Urban Development
http://www.stadtentwicklung.berlin.de/index_en.shtml
Information on planning, housing, environmental policy, and future projects taking place in Berlin. This site also has a section on monuments in Berlin, including a comprehensive feature on the remains of the Berlin Wall.

Books

Dahlberg, Maurine. *Escape to West Berlin.* New York: Farrar, Straus & Giroux, 2004. A novel about a family divided by the construction of the Berlin Wall.

Donaldson, Gerry, and Sonja Schantz. *Countries of the World: Germany.* New York: Facts On File, 2004. An introduction to the country as a whole, including its large cities.

Eyewitness Travel Guides: Berlin. New York: Dorling Kindersley, 2006. A highly illustrated guide to Berlin containing some cultural and historical background.

Funder, Anna. *Stasiland.* London: Granta, 2003. An award-winning and moving book about the effect the East German secret police had on the lives of ordinary people in East Germany.

Isherwood, Christopher. *Goodbye to Berlin.* London: Vintage, 1989. A fascinating portrait of the city's people and lifestyle just before Hitler came to power; first published in 1939.

Richie, Alexandra. *Faust's Metropolis.* New York: Carroll & Graf, 1999. A detailed history of Berlin from its origins to the present day.

Time Out: Berlin. 7th ed. London: Time Out Guides, 2006. A comprehensive travel guide to Berlin with inside information on the city and a good section on its history.

Index